Arjun's Duty

Bhagavad Gita for Kids

Volume I

Illustrated by Kevin Flager

© 2022 Simit Patel
All rights reserved.
www.hindukidbooks.com

Paperback ISBN: 978-0-578-34898-8
Ebook ISBN: 978-0-578-34899-5

Illustrations by Kevin Flager
Book design by Sarah E. Holroyd (https://sleepingcatbooks.com)

The Gita is not a book of commands, but a book of choices.

— Vyasa (author of the Gita)

A long time ago, in the land of Kurukshetra, there lived a prince named Arjun. He had four other brothers. His father, Pandu, was the king, and his mother, Kunti, was the queen. Arjun and his four brothers were known as the Pandavs. They had over a hundred cousins, who were known as the Kauravs.

The Pandavs and Kauravs studied together. One of their teachers, Drona, worked with the Pandavs and Kauravs to help them learn the art of war to defend the people of Kurukshetra. Drona focused on teaching them how to focus, so that they would be skilled in using a bow and arrow. Drona thought Arjun was the best at focusing his mind, and so the best at using his bow and arrow.

But there were problems in Kurukshetra. Both the Pandavs and the Kauravs wanted to inherit the kingdom of Kurukshetra from King Pandu and Queen Kunti. Arjun and his brothers believed that they were the children of the King and Queen, and thus saw themselves as the rightful heirs to the kingdom. The Kauravs, though, wanted the kingdom for themselves. They were jealous that the Pandavs were the next to be kings. They were jealous of Arjun's skill with his bow and arrow.

One day, Shakuni, an uncle on the Kauravs side, came up with a plan to steal the kingdom of Kurkshetra from the Pandavs. He invited the oldest Pandav, Yudhishthira, to play a game of dice with him. "Come play dice with your cousin Duryodhana," Shakuni said. He then whispered to his nephew Duryodhana the real plan. "We will roll trick dice," he said. "That way, we will trick Yudhishthira into gambling everything he has away!"

So Shakuni called Yudhishthira over to play dice, and Yudhishthira came. Since Shakuni was using trick dice, Yudhishthira kept losing. At first, the losses were small. But Yudishthira was getting upset and scared. He did not want to lose more of his possessions, and he wanted more of what Shakuni had.

Shakuni could see that Yudishthira was not calm. He knew this was his chance to steal the kingdom. "Okay Yudhishthira, on this roll of the dice I would like to gamble even more. If you win, you can have anything of mine that you would like. But if I win, the Pandavs must leave Kurukshetra for 12 years. The Kauravs will rule Kurukshetra during that time. The Pandavs can return as kings after the 12 years have passed."

Yudhishthira looked around nervously. He wanted to win, and he wanted the things that Shakuni had. He agreed to Shakuni's offer.

Shakuni smiled. He rolled the dice, knowing what would happen. The trick dice worked in his favor. The Pandavs would be forced to leave, and the Kauravs would be kings for the next 12 years!

Yudishthira was devastated. He had wanted what Shakuni had so much that he ended up losing everything. He knew, though, that he must honor his word and leave Kurukshetra. So he faced his brothers the Pandavs, and they all agreed to leave Kurukshetra for 12 years. They abandoned their palace, and went to live in the forest.

While on their forest, the Pandavs had time to think about what had happened. Arjun thought to stop by to see Lord Krishna, the God who had created the whole world, to help him understand what had occurred. "Why did this happen to us? What are we to do?"

Krishna could see that Arjun was worried and troubled. He sought to console Arjun with the truth of the matter. "It is your desires that have brought you sadness and pain," Krishna said. "Yudhishthira wanted what Shakuni had. When you want what others have, you can find yourself sad and angry. Instead, want only to tell the truth and live with love. When you are close to truth and to love, you are close to me. Then you will be happy and at peace, no matter what else is happening."

Finally, after twelve years in solitude, Arjun, Yudhishthira, and the rest of the Pandavs returned to Kurukshetra. "We have come back after our exile. We have honored the terms of the dice game. It is time for us to reclaim the kingdom."

Duryodhana sneered. "Ha! You fools. The kingdom is ours and will remain as such. We will not give it back to you. It is ours!" He cackled and gave an evil grin to the Pandavs.

The Pandavs were growing anxious and concerned. What were they to do now? Yudhishthira decided to make an offer to Durodhyana. "Just give us 5 villages, and you can have the rest of Kurukshetra," he said. But Duryodhana refused. He wanted the entire kingdom for the Kauravs. "No!" He said. "Either the Pandavs go, or the Kauravs go. But we will not share the kingdom with you!" he said angrily.

Duryodhana could see that the Pandavs did not like this response, and that they might not simply walk away from the kingdom. He thought he may need to use force and fight them to get them to leave. With that in mind, he went to see Lord Krishna, to ask for his help in getting the Pandavs to leave Kurukshetra.

Duryodhana arrived first to see Lord Krishna, and Arjun arrived shortly after. Both found Lord Krishna sleeping, and waited patiently for him to awake. When he woke up, he saw Arjun first. Duryodhana and Arjun explained to Lord Krishna that a battle over the kingdom of Kurukshetra was likely to happen. Arjun came to ask for Lord Krishna's help, as did Duryodhana.

Krishna looked at both Duryodhana and Arjun. He said, "I will help you both. But since I saw Arjun first when I woke up, and since he is the younger of you two, I will give him the first choice." Lord Krishna turned to Arjun. "Arjun, I will give you two choices. The first choice is that you can have my army of 1 million soldiers, the yadava soldiers. They are the best fighters in the world, with the most powerful weapons. The second choice is that you can have me on your side. I will not fight and will not bring any weapons. But I will give you my guidance."

Arjun thought for a moment. He knew his duty was to have faith in Lord Krishna, and to trust him. But he was scared. If he chose Lord Krishna, Duryodhana would get the army of powerful yadava soldiers. What should he do?

Finally, he responded. "Lord Krishna, I choose you." Duryodhana jumped for joy and laughed in delight. "You fool!" he said to Arjun. "Now the Kauravs will definitely win!" Duryodhana left Lord Krishna, convinced his army of 1 million yadava soldiers would help him win the Kurukshetra War.

And so, the next day, the Kurukshetra War began. As Arjun rode in his chariot to the battle, with Krishna by his side, he began to cry. "Lord Krishna, how can I do this?

How can I fight my cousins? I am very sad and disturbed by this." Lord Krishna calmly replied, "Arjun, remember that you must only consider your duty in this life. It is your duty to defend the Pandavs and the people. You are on the side that is right and good, and it is your duty to stand for what is right and what is good."

Arjun calmed down a bit, thinking about what Lord Krishna had told him. But he was still a bit concerned. "But what about the pain I will cause others? And what about the pain I will bring to myself?" Krishna smiled and told him, "Arjun, remember who you are. Remember who each one of us is. You are not your body. Your body is just like your clothes. By this I mean it is like an outer dress, or a costume.

Your **atma**, or your soul, is who you really are. And your Atma cannot be hurt. It was alive since the beginning, and it will be alive after this body dies. Because of this, you can rest knowing that you cannot truly hurt yourself or others. You are here in this life only to do your duty. When you pursue your duty with all your heart, you will experience the peace you are looking for."

Arjun smiled. Finally, he understood the situation. Armed with the truth he had received from Lord Krishna, he went to fulfill his duty and defend his people in the Kurukshetra War. In doing so, he found his peace, and helped the people in the kingdom of Kurukshetra win and live happily.

Milton Keynes UK
Ingram Content Group UK Ltd.
UKHW020404181023
430805UK00005B/31